Arts and Crafts
of
ANCIENT ROME

Ting Morris

Illustrated by Emma Young

W

FRANKLIN WATTS
LONDON•SYDNEY

An Appleseed Editions book

First published in 2006 by Franklin Watts
338 Euston Road, London NW1 3BH

Franklin Watts Australia, Hachette Children's Books
Level 17/207 Kent Street, Sydney, NSW 2000

© 2006 Appleseed Editions

Created by Appleseed Editions Ltd, Well House,
Friars Hill, Guestling, East Sussex TN35 4ET

Artwork by Emma Young
Designed by Helen James
Edited by Mary-Jane Wilkins
Picture research by Su Alexander

ISBN 0 7496 6743 5

Dewey Classification: 704.03'81

A CIP catalogue for this book is available from the British Library

Photograph acknowledgements
Front cover copyright The Trustees of The British Museum; page 5t
copyright The Trustees of The British Museum, b Archivo Iconografico,
S.A./Corbis; 6 Araldo de Luca/Corbis; 7 Archivo Iconografico, S.A./Corbis;
8 Vanni Archive/Corbis; 9t Vittoriano Rastelli/Corbis, b Archivo Iconografico,
S.A./Corbis; 10 Roger Wood/Corbis; 12 Massimo Listri/Corbis; 13 Werner
Forman/Corbis; 14 Archivo Iconografico, S.A./Corbis; 15t Gianni Dagli
Orti/Corbis, b Mimmo Jodice/Corbis; 16 Chris Hellier/Corbis; 18 Alinari
Archives/Corbis; 19, 20, 21 & 22 copyright The Trustees of The British
Museum; 24 Adam Woolfitt/Corbis; 25 copyright The Trustees of The British
Museum; 26 Archivo Iconografico, S.A./Corbis; 27 copyright The Trustees
of The British Museum; 28 Mimmo Jodice/Corbis:

Printed in Singapore

Contents

The world of the ancient Romans   4

Roman sculpture   6

Carved in relief   8

Make a relief   10

Wall painting   12

The art of mosaic   14

Make your own mosaic   16

Metalwork   18

Pottery and terracotta   20

Make a Roman vase   22

Working with glass   24

Gems and jewellery   26

Make some jewellery   28

Glossary   30

Index   32

The world of the ancient Romans

Rome began around 2800 years ago as a few small settlements on wooded hills overlooking the River Tiber. Over the centuries it grew into a small kingdom, but around 500 BC its citizens decided that they would be better off without an all-powerful king. Rome became a republic, which meant that the citizens chose their leaders.

By 270 BC the Roman Republic had taken over all Italy, and the army leaders were fighting for power. Julius Caesar seized power in 46 BC, and 19 years later his adopted son became the first Roman emperor, naming himself Augustus. Millions of people came under Roman rule and the empire soon dominated Europe, North Africa and the Middle East. Then in AD 476 Germanic invaders sacked Rome and overthrew its emperor.

The Roman Empire (green on this map) was largest around AD 120. It stretched for thousands of kilometres from its capital in central Italy.

Romulus and Remus

According to legend, Rome was founded in 753 BC by Romulus, who gave the city its name. Baby Romulus and his twin brother Remus were the sons of Rhea Silvia and Mars, the god of war. The story tells how their uncle put the baby brothers in a basket and cast them adrift on the River Tiber. The boys were washed to the riverbank and a she-wolf heard the babies' cries and suckled them. Then a shepherd found them and took them home. He and his wife brought them up as their own sons. When the boys were older, they decided to found a city on the hills beside the river. But they argued over who was to rule the city, and Romulus killed his brother.

Building an empire

The Romans built such a large and successful empire that their culture and traditions reached all parts of the Mediterranean region. They took them as far north as Britain. An excellent network of Roman roads meant that their special skills, including craft techniques and artistic styles, spread throughout Europe and influenced many other people. Ancient Roman artists celebrated the success of their expanding empire with great skill.

This terracotta panel was made around AD 200. It shows two prisoners being led through the streets of Rome in an open cart. Panels like this decorated the walls of some Roman houses.

This bronze sculpture of the she-wolf was made soon after 500 BC. The suckling twins were added later. The sculpture has become the symbol of Rome.

Roman sculpture

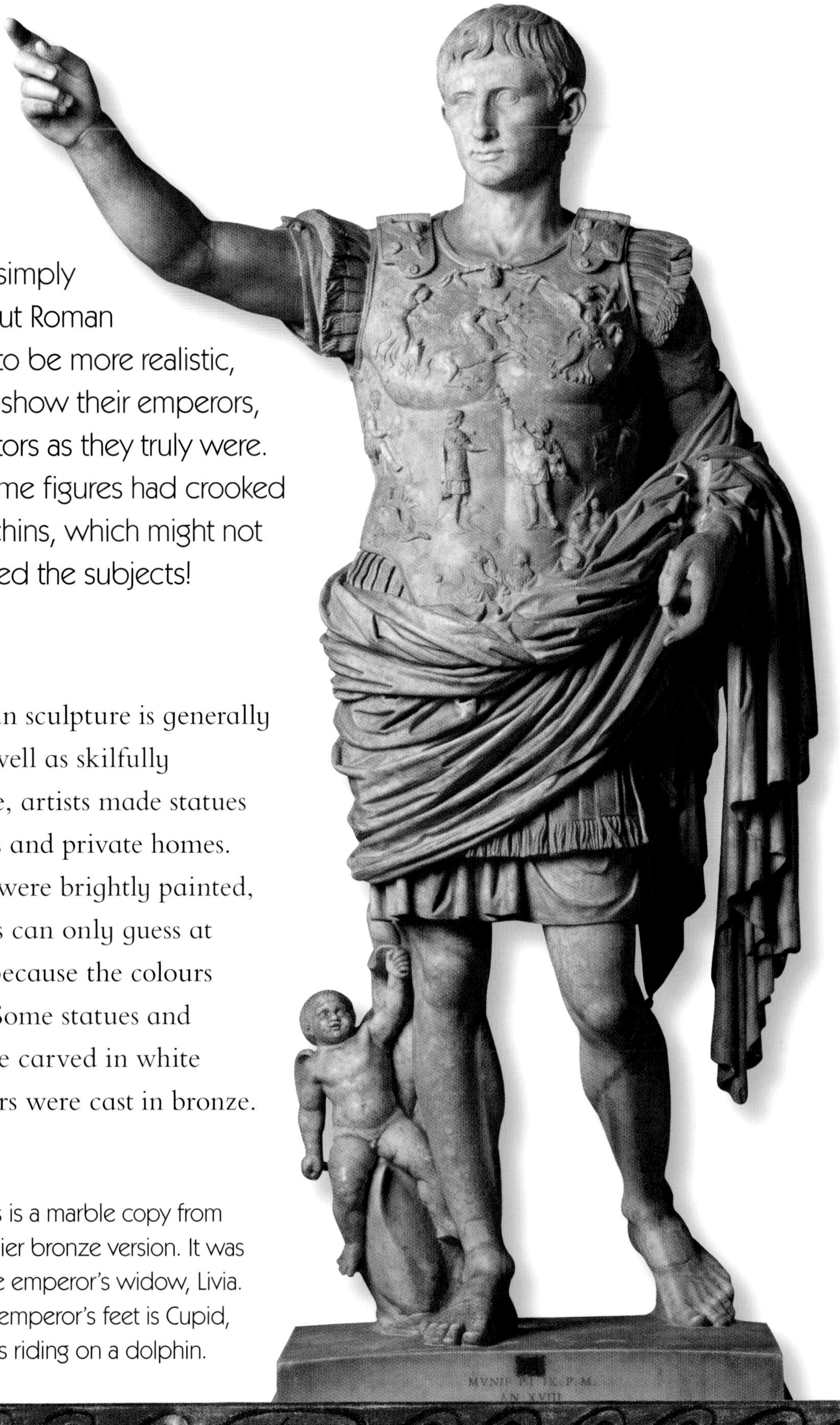

The style of ancient Greek sculpture had a great influence on the Romans, who simply copied it at first. But Roman sculptors wanted to be more realistic, and many tried to show their emperors, generals and senators as they truly were. This meant that some figures had crooked noses or double chins, which might not always have pleased the subjects!

Despite this, Roman sculpture is generally very beautiful, as well as skilfully produced. In Rome, artists made statues for public buildings and private homes. Most stone statues were brightly painted, but modern experts can only guess at how they looked, because the colours have worn away. Some statues and smaller figures were carved in white marble, while others were cast in bronze.

This statue of Augustus is a marble copy from about AD 15 of an earlier bronze version. It was found at the villa of the emperor's widow, Livia. The small figure at the emperor's feet is Cupid, the god of love, who is riding on a dolphin.

First emperor

By the time of the empire there was a great demand for sculptures to honour the emperor and other important people. The sculptures were put up in public squares, halls and temples, and some were even placed on top of columns. The idea was to show the power of the empire. Many statues were made of the first emperor, Augustus (who ruled 27 BC–AD 14), and most made him look like a young hero. In the famous example left, he is speaking to his soldiers after a great victory.

Imperial ladies

Roman sculptors portrayed women far less often than men. This was because women had little to do with running or defending the empire. However, female members of the imperial household – especially the wife and daughters of the emperor – made good subjects. Male sculptors and female subjects took the opportunity to show off new, fashionable hairstyles.

This marble bust of a lady comes from the period of the Flavian family of Roman emperors, who ruled from AD 69 to 96.

Carved in relief

Roman sculptors liked to work in relief. This meant carving their figures or designs so that they stood out from a stone background. They used this method to tell the story of historical events in beautifully designed friezes, or bands of relief sculpture.

You can still see some famous examples in Rome today. One is the Ara Pacis (Altar of Peace), which the Roman senate had made in 13 BC. This monumental marble altar has carvings that celebrate the return of Emperor Augustus from his campaigns in Spain and Gaul, and the peace that followed. The reliefs show members of his family, as well as scenes from Roman myths and legends. Experts think that the sculptors of the altar were Greek. It was certainly carved in the ancient Greek tradition.

Telling a story

Trajan's Column is one of Rome's greatest monuments. The 30-metre high circular column commemorates the victory over the Dacians by the Emperor Trajan (who ruled AD 98–117). The Dacian people lived in what is now Romania, and Trajan made their territory a province of the Roman empire.

The column is made of 20 blocks of marble, and covered with a strip of reliefs that spiral to the top. The idea was that people would see the upper parts from

Part of the outside marble enclosure of the Altar of Peace. The upper section tells a story from Roman mythology, and the frieze below is made up of a beautiful floral decoration. The altar inside the enclosure was used for sacrificing animals to the gods.

Trajan's Column is like an ancient cartoon strip. The frieze band is more than a metre high, and scenes are divided by a tree or rock.

the galleries of library buildings that stood around the column. A statue of the emperor stood on top, and his ashes were buried underneath.

Everyday life

Archaeologists have found Roman reliefs and other sculptures all around the Mediterranean region. These finds have helped us to understand what life was like in ancient times. As well as making reliefs of victorious battles, sculptors sometimes chose everyday events as their subjects. One relief found in Bodrum, in modern Turkey, shows female gladiators fighting with swords and shields. Others show Roman streets, craftsmen at work and even shops.

This 2nd-century relief shows a Roman butcher chopping meat in his shop.

Make a relief

Roman sculptures can be in high relief or low relief. If they stand out a long way, they are in high relief. When you look at the friezes on Trajan's Column, you can see that figures in the background are in lower relief than those in the foreground. This helps to give the viewer a sense of distance.

The three gorgons were monstrous sisters in Greek mythology. The Romans believed in them too. This gorgon head comes from the top of an arch in the Roman city of Leptis Magna, in present-day Libya. It was put there to scare away other monsters and evil spirits.

To make a Gorgon head

You will need: 4 cups plain flour • 2 cups fine salt • 1–2 cups lukewarm water • a large mixing bowl • a large plate • a small plate • a modelling tool • a lolly stick • a toothpick • white ready-mixed paint • poster paints • paintbrushes • clear varnish or varnish spray • a baking tray • aluminium foil

1 This relief is made with salt-dough. Mix the flour and salt together in a large bowl. Add the water to the mixture. Knead with your hands until the dough is soft, but not sticky. If the mixture is too dry, add more water (a few drops at a time). If it feels too wet, add more flour. Knead for 5 minutes until the dough is smooth.

2 Roll out a large lump of dough to about 2 cm thick. Place the large plate on it and cut around it to make the outer circle. Roll out more dough and cut around the smaller plate to make the face.

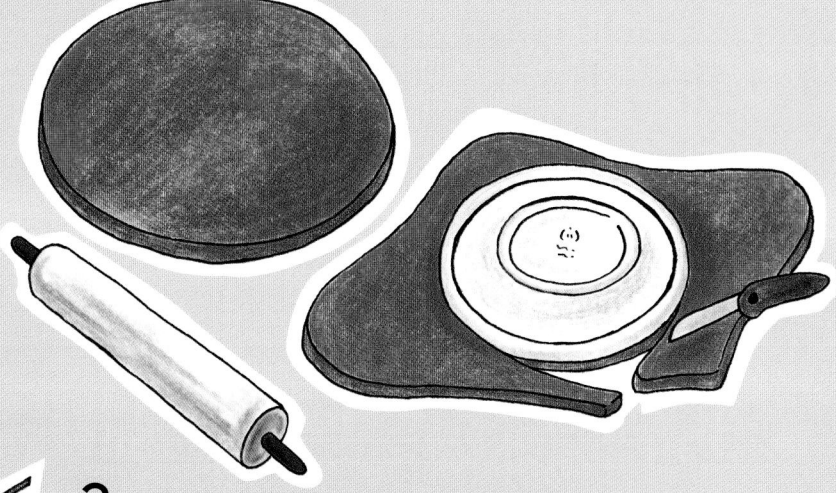

3 Stick the smaller circle on to the larger one. Dip a paintbrush in water, wet the facing sides and gently press them together. Make a hole with a toothpick at the top of the outer circle, so you can hang up the finished relief.

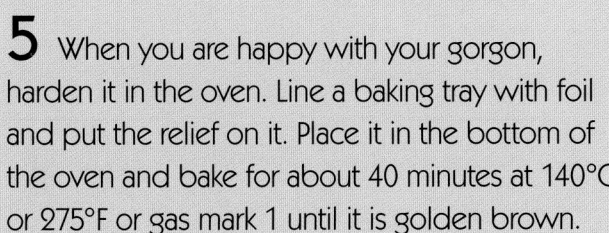

4 Model eyebrows and lips with dough coils. Make dough balls for the eyes and nose and stick them on with a little water. Shape scary features for the gorgon with a modelling tool and fingers. Roll out thin dough sausages for her curly hair. Moisten the coils and stick them on the outer circle so the hair surrounds the face.

5 When you are happy with your gorgon, harden it in the oven. Line a baking tray with foil and put the relief on it. Place it in the bottom of the oven and bake for about 40 minutes at 140°C or 275°F or gas mark 1 until it is golden brown.

6 When it has cooled, paint the relief with white ready-mixed paint. Once dry, use poster paint to give it the colour of stone. You can colour the hair, eyes and lips – ancient sculptures were usually painted. Finish with a coat of varnish. Put a string through the hole and hang up the relief where evil spirits may lurk. Your gorgon will scare them away!

Wall painting

There were many wall paintings on public buildings in ancient Rome. But from about 100 BC the Romans also decorated the walls inside their houses. They probably did this to make rooms look bigger and more interesting.

Most of the wall paintings were made on damp plaster. These frescoes were brightly coloured and lasted well. Artists liked to paint the legendary adventures of gods, heroes and heroines, as well as animals and landscapes. They also painted portraits of living people on the walls of their houses. We know about the different styles from paintings found at Pompeii and other towns that were buried under volcanic ash when Mount Vesuvius erupted in AD 79.

Developing styles

Historians divide the paintings found at Pompeii and elsewhere into four different styles. In the first style, artists painted walls to look as if they were made of slabs of shiny marble. In the second,

This painting from a house in Pompeii shows a woman performing mysterious rites in honour of Dionysus, the god of wine (also called Bacchus).

they painted scenes as if the viewer was looking through a window. The pictures portrayed realistic people on brilliant red backgrounds, and painted black columns often acted as frames.

The third style, which dates from about 15 BC, made walls into a picture gallery of large and small, more delicate paintings. The fourth style combined the previous two and had more variations.

Decorated bedrooms

We know from a famous example at Boscoreale, another town buried by the eruption of Vesuvius, that Roman artists decorated whole rooms with paintings. A bedroom from the villa of Publius Fannius Synistor has been reconstructed in a museum, and it shows that the Romans had frescoes as some people today have wallpaper. The room has a small real window, but other panels are painted with views of courtyards, countryside and the town – as if the people in the room were looking out of large windows. This gives the feeling of a much bigger space.

This reconstructed bedroom from Boscoreale, was originally painted around 40 BC in the second style.

The art of mosaic

Mosaics are small pieces of stone, tile, glass or other hard material arranged to form a design or picture. This art form probably began in ancient Mesopotamia (modern Iraq), and was taken up by the Greeks. Roman artists learned the technique from Greek master craftsmen, and they began making their own around the 2nd century BC.

Mosaic pieces were usually cube-shaped, and the Romans called them tesserae (meaning cubes). Early patterns were black and white, and covered whole floors. Then artists introduced coloured materials, and laid complicated pictures to go with wall paintings. By the 1st century AD, artists were designing mosaics for walls and ceilings too.

Planning and designing

Only wealthy house-owners could afford to hire a team of craftsmen to lay a mosaic in one of the main rooms of their house. First an artist drew the chosen design, before passing it to the craftworker responsible for producing the thousands of tesserae needed for the finished mosaic.

This detailed floor mosaic was found in one of the houses buried at Pompeii. It shows actors getting ready to perform a play.

Mosaic cubes were usually 1 to 1.5 cm square. Craft workers used ironstone for red cubes, sandstone for yellow, slate for blue and chalk for white. The craftsman who laid the mosaic put the cubes close together in a bed of fresh mortar, then filled the spaces between with fine mortar. When this had set, the mosaic was cleaned and polished.

This mosaic at the entrance of a Roman house was a warning. It read Cave canem, or Beware of the dog!

This geometric mosaic covered the floor of a room in a bathing house.

Impressive and practical

House-owners could buy some designs ready-made from workshops, but each mosaic had to be individually fitted to a room or space. The finished mosaic was meant to impress visitors. At the same time, mosaics made very practical flooring in Italy and other warm lands around the Mediterranean. They were hard-wearing and long-lasting. Mosaics are still popular today, though larger tiles are easier and cheaper to lay.

Make your own mosaic

Some Roman rooms had a plain floor with a mosaic picture in the middle. Mosaic designs were copied from Greek and Roman paintings. Later, these centrepieces were also used outdoors, in pavements.

This fish formed part of a mosaic at the Roman city of Anazarbus, in modern Turkey.

Make a fish mosaic

You will need: air-hardening clay
• card and paper 18 x 12 cm • a rolling
pin • two 1-cm thick pieces of wood
• a modelling knife • a ruler • acrylic
or poster paints • double-sided tape
• PVA glue • flour • paintbrushes
• colouring pencils • a pencil

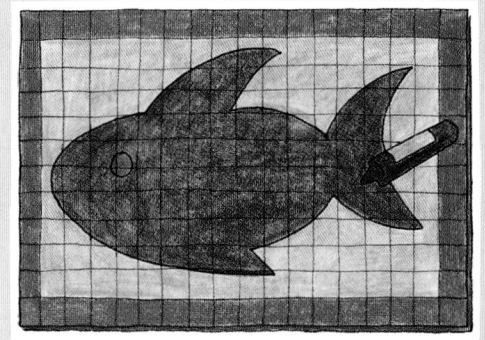

1 Sketch out the design in colour on paper. Plan your mosaic and work out how many tesserae you'll need. You can use any size pieces, squares or random shapes. If you make a mosaic with 1-cm tiles, multiply the width by the length of the paper. For this 18 x 12 cm fish mosaic you will need 216 clay tiles. Copy the fish on to the card.

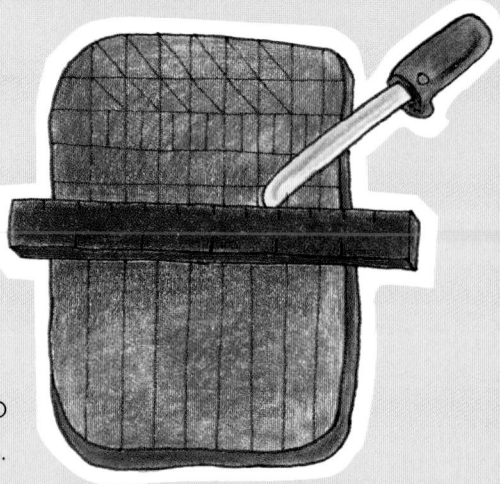

2 Roll out two balls of clay using wood pieces on either side as guides. Leave to firm up for 10 minutes. Use a ruler as a guide and cut horizontal and vertical lines 1 cm apart, making small clay squares. Cut them out with a modelling knife. You'll need 216 for the fish, but cut a number of tiles into smaller shapes and triangles for fillers. Let them dry for 24 hours.

3 Paint the pieces using different colours. You'll need blue tiles for the sea, and red tiles for the fish, as well as orange border tiles. Paint some of the small shapes black to make eyes and mouth. Leave to dry.

4 Arrange the tiles on the card. Start with the fish. Use double-sided tape to check that the shapes fit. When you have assembled the pieces for one section, glue them in place. Spread on the adhesive and press in the pieces, a small part at a time.

5 Build up the border with orange tiles and fill in the water with blue tesserae. Fill the gaps between tiles with PVA glue thickened with flour. You can colour this with a little poster paint.

6 Finally, apply a thick coat of PVA glue all over the tiles. Use a big paintbrush for an even finish. Leave to dry overnight.

Metalwork

A mixture of copper and tin called bronze was the best and most popular metal for Roman sculpture. Metalworkers cast molten bronze to make large statues as well as small figurines of people and animals. They also made bronze models of chariots and other objects.

Most works were cast by the lost-wax method. First the sculptor shaped the statue in wax around a clay core. He covered the wax in a layer of clay, and heated the sculpture. The wax melted and ran out, leaving a gap into which the sculptor poured molten bronze. The bronze took the shape of the wax. When it was cool, the sculptor removed the clay shape.

Large statues were made in separate pieces, which were joined together with molten lead and bronze. Few bronze statues still stand, because most were melted down so that the metal could be reused.

Furniture and tableware

Bronze was not used just for statues, tools and weapons – many furnishings in Roman homes were made from it. Tables, benches and chairs had

This bronze statue of Emperor Marcus Aurelius, who ruled from AD 161 to 180, is a copy of the original. It stands in the Capitoline Square in Rome. The original statue has been moved to a museum.

bronze legs, and bronze lamps and lanterns lit houses. Gold and silver were made into more precious objects, including beautiful tableware. Many wealthy families had silverware for special occasions, marked with their name. Gold and silver objects were decorated by beating out a design from the inside.

From the Temple of Juno

The Roman mint, where metal coins were made, was in a building that stood next to the Temple of Juno. In Roman mythology, Juno was the wife of Jupiter and the goddess of marriage and childbirth. Her temple was dedicated to her under the name Juno Moneta, which meant Juno the counsellor.

Historians believe that as the Romans made their coins near there, *moneta* came to mean this, and our word money comes from the Latin term. The first Roman coins were rough lumps of bronze, and the first silver coins came into use in 269 BC.

The front and back of a Roman silver denarius coin. The front has a portrait of Juno, and the back shows metalworking tools – tongs, an anvil and a hammer. The coin dates from 46 BC, when Julius Caesar was the most powerful man in Rome.

Pottery and terracotta

Greek potters had a great influence on the artists and craftworkers of ancient Rome. Roman potters followed earlier Greek techniques and styles. They worked at a fast-turning wheel to turn lumps of clay into pots, jars, vases and all sorts of other containers.

Some of the pots were made for practical use, such as the large jars called *amphorae*, which stored wine or olive oil. Others were decorative as well, such as the jugs with delicate handles which carried liquid to the table or banquet.

The Romans learned to use moulds, so that pots could be made more easily and quickly. This led to an early form of mass production. Many different objects were made of terracotta (meaning baked earth), or clay fired in a kiln, or oven. These included decorative panels and lamps.

This terracotta mask shows the face of a tragic character from a Roman play. It was made around AD 100, probably to be used as an offering, rather than to be worn.

Sealed clay from Arretium

From about 30 BC, some of the finest Roman pottery was made in the town of Arretium (modern Arezzo, in Tuscany). There potters began mass-producing pottery with a shiny red finish. This is called Arretine ware or sealed clay, and the pots are often covered with decorated reliefs.

The designs were made in moulds that were attached to the potter's wheel. Master potters ran workshops in and around Arretium, helped by assistants, apprentices and slaves. Their skilful work became known throughout the Roman world.

Oil lamps

The Romans had candles and lanterns, but the most popular form of lighting was oil-burning lamps. Most lamps were made of terracotta and burned olive oil. Lamps also needed a wick, which might have been made of linen or papyrus.

This terracotta lamp shows a chariot race in the Circus Maximus stadium in Rome. The hole near the middle is for pouring oil into the lamp. The wick passed through the hole in the nozzle.

Make a Roman vase

Roman vases were used for many purposes. Large amphora containers could store about 23 litres of wine or oil, but some vases were simply pieces of art or ornaments.

This funny vase was made around AD 200 in Cnidus (in modern Turkey). It is 17 cm high and the clay was pressed into a mould with two parts. The halves were then joined and the details added by hand. It was probably a caricature of a real person.

Make a funny vase

You will need: air-drying clay • a rolling pin • two 1-cm thick pieces of wood • a board • a modelling knife • 2 small bowls (foil or plastic) • cling film • water • purple acrylic paint (or poster paint and varnish) • a small sponge • paintbrushes • a toothpick

1 Roll out the clay, using the pieces of wood on either side as a thickness guide. Place one bowl upside down on the slab and cut around it. Make the circle a little bigger than the bowl.

2 Roll out another slab and cut around the bowl as before. Cut out a small round hole for the top of the vase. Line the bowls with cling film and press the two circles inside. Allow the clay to harden slightly in the moulds. It will stiffen more quickly if you use a hairdryer for 5 minutes.

3 Score the outer edges of the clay circles and moisten them with a damp sponge. Press the two bowls together with the clay still inside. The bowl with the cut-out hole should be on top.

4 Once the clay is firm but not completely dry, it will hold its shape. Take off the bowls. Pinch the clay rim together and smooth the edges where the sides meet. Place a coil around the hole in the top. If you want handles, make two more coils. Score and moisten the clay before pressing on the coils.

5 Mould a big triangle of clay for the nose and press a pencil into it to make nostrils. Make balls for eyes and coils for lips and eyebrows. Draw details with a toothpick. Roll out thin clay sausages for hair, and don't forget the ears. Score and moisten the clay whenever you add anything. Leave the vase to dry, then paint it.

Working with glass

Glass vessels were very popular in Roman times. From the 1st century BC many containers were made of glass rather than pottery. Glass was also used to make window panes, and small pieces of glass were used in mosaics and decorative wall panels.

The artistic and practical use of glass changed around 50 BC everywhere in the ancient world. This was when glass-blowing was invented, probably in the region of present-day Syria. The new technique soon reached Rome, and glass objects were no longer a luxury. The skilful glassmaker dipped a hollow blowpipe into molten glass and then blew into the pipe to make the glass bulge out and form a hollow shape. He then stretched and squeezed the glass into the shape he wanted.

An expert looks at an 18th-century plaster copy as he restores the original Portland Vase. The scene on the vase is the wedding of mythical King Peleus and the sea-nymph Thetis.

The Portland Vase

Roman glassmakers learned how to build up different-coloured layers of glass and then cut designs in relief. The dark blue and white Portland Vase is a perfect example of this art, and it is one of the most famous and valuable glass objects in the world.

The vase was probably made in Rome at the beginning of the 1st century AD. More than 1700 years later the Duke of Portland bought it. He sold it to the British Museum, which put the vase on display in London. A museum visitor smashed the vase to pieces in 1845, but it has since been put back together and restored.

Mould-blowing

Glassmakers made beakers and other vessels by blowing the molten glass into a carved clay mould. This was much quicker than making free-blown glass. The mould had to be made first, but then could be used many times in a form of mass production. All sorts of designs and images were used, including sporting events, so that the glassware could be kept as a souvenir.

This glass beaker was found at Camulodunum, the Roman town that became Colchester, in south-east England. It shows a race with four horse-drawn chariots. It even names the winner: a charioteer named Cresces beat Antilochus into second place.

Gems and jewellery

Roman women valued gems and precious stones for their magic and healing qualities, as well as for their beauty. Gold and silver jewellery was very popular, and gemstones included cornelian, amethyst and sapphire, which was brought from faraway India.

Wealthy women liked to wear bracelets, necklaces, anklets, pendants, rings and earrings. Those who could not afford these wore similar jewellery made of coloured glass. Men generally didn't wear jewellery, apart from a signet ring with a carved gemstone that acted as a seal when stamped in clay or wax. Some rings were iron or silver, and men of high status had gold signet rings with valuable jewels. Rome's leading gem-cutters were Greeks, and the most skilful jewellers signed or marked their works.

Cameos

Ancient Greek craftsmen were the first to make the engraved gems that we call cameos. The Romans also learned this art. They used a gemstone called chalcedony, which has layers of different colours.

Free-born Roman children wore a pendant around their neck, called a bulla, for protection and good luck. This one is made of gold. Boys wore their bulla until they were old enough to wear an adult toga. Girls wore theirs until they married.

This cameo of the first emperor, Augustus, was cut from a three-layered sardonyx (a kind of chalcedony). The jewelled headband was added after Roman times.

Gem-cutters delicately carved a design into the top layer, so that it stood out in relief. They created portraits of emperors and other important Romans, sometimes setting the stone in an oval frame of gold.

Hoards of gold

The Romans buried hoards of gold and precious items around their empire, including their most northerly province – Britain. One example is the treasure found at Hoxne, Suffolk, in 1992. The finder was looking for his friend's lost hammer! The hoard contained thousands of gold and silver coins, as well as gold rings (with the gemstones removed), necklaces, pendants, bracelets and chains. Experts believe that the hoard was buried around AD 400, when Britain was passing out of Roman control.

Make some jewellery

Merchants brought back precious stones from all parts of the growing empire. This meant that Roman jewellers had good supplies of emeralds, amethysts, sapphires and uncut diamonds. They used long rows of gems as beads or put them in delicate gold settings.

Some beautiful jewellery and ivory pins found at Pompeii. The bracelet at the front is made of hollow gold beads.

Make your own jewellery

You will need: pasta shapes (short and long tubes, wheels)
• elastic • red, blue, green and purple poster paints • a small brush • florist's wire or fine copper wire • gold paper (or gift wrap) • two toothpicks • varnish (PVA glue mixed with a little water) • an apple • strong glue.

1 To make the gems, colour the pasta shapes with poster paints and felt pens. Wait for the paint to dry before varnishing the shapes. Cut 120 cm of elastic for your necklace.

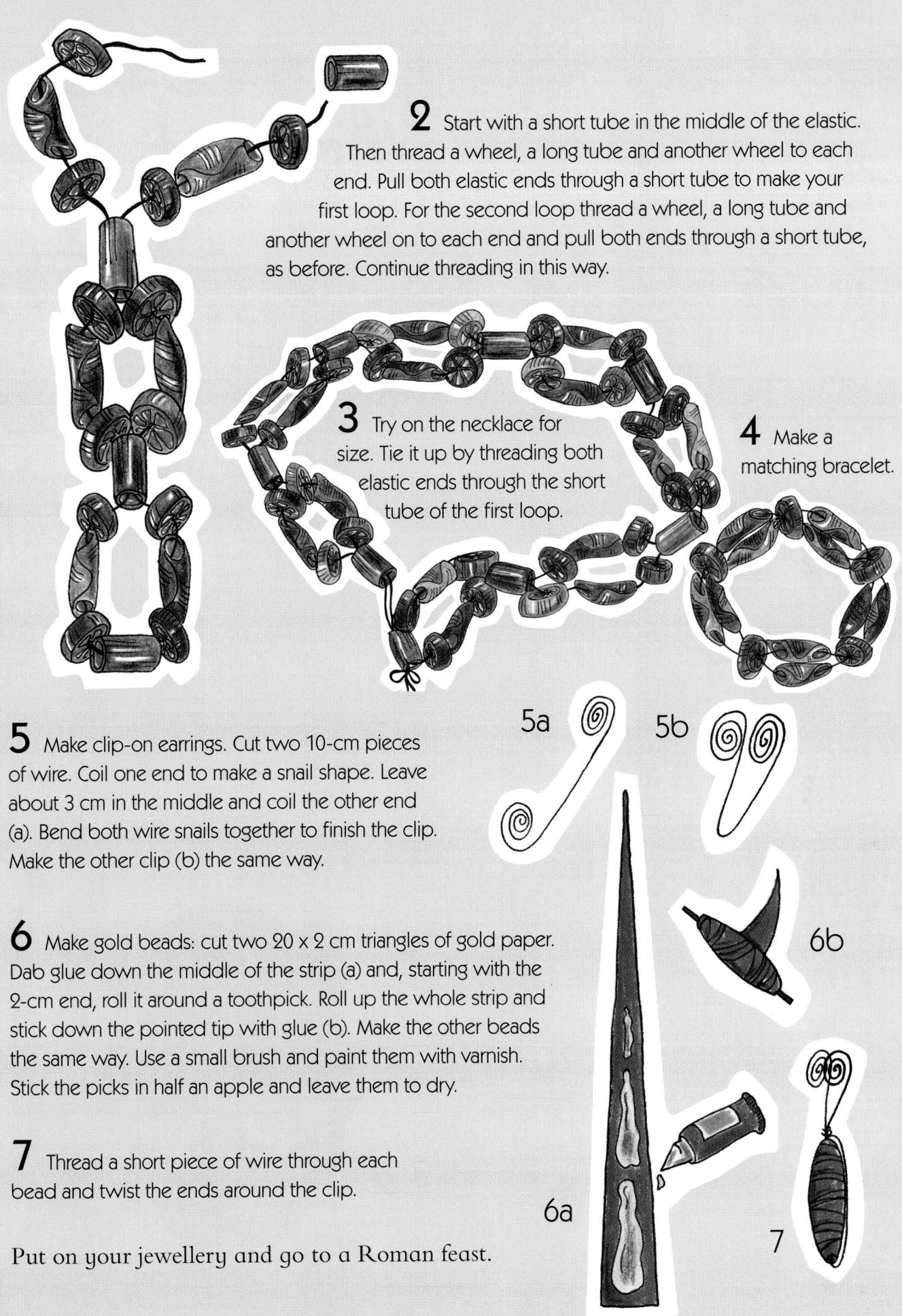

2 Start with a short tube in the middle of the elastic. Then thread a wheel, a long tube and another wheel to each end. Pull both elastic ends through a short tube to make your first loop. For the second loop thread a wheel, a long tube and another wheel on to each end and pull both ends through a short tube, as before. Continue threading in this way.

3 Try on the necklace for size. Tie it up by threading both elastic ends through the short tube of the first loop.

4 Make a matching bracelet.

5 Make clip-on earrings. Cut two 10-cm pieces of wire. Coil one end to make a snail shape. Leave about 3 cm in the middle and coil the other end (a). Bend both wire snails together to finish the clip. Make the other clip (b) the same way.

6 Make gold beads: cut two 20 x 2 cm triangles of gold paper. Dab glue down the middle of the strip (a) and, starting with the 2-cm end, roll it around a toothpick. Roll up the whole strip and stick down the pointed tip with glue (b). Make the other beads the same way. Use a small brush and paint them with varnish. Stick the picks in half an apple and leave them to dry.

7 Thread a short piece of wire through each bead and twist the ends around the clip.

Put on your jewellery and go to a Roman feast.

Glossary

amphora A tall jar with two handles used for storing wine and other liquids.

archaeologist A person who studies the ancient past by digging up and looking at remains.

bronze A metal that is a mixture of copper and tin.

bust A sculpture of a person's head and shoulders.

cameo A piece of jewellery made by carving a gemstone to give a raised design in a different colour from the background.

figurine A small figure or statuette.

fresco A wall painting made on damp plaster.

frieze A band of sculpture or painting high on a wall.

gladiator A fighter trained to battle with other fighters or wild animals in an arena.

hoard A hidden store of treasure.

imperial To do with an empire, emperor or empress.

kiln An oven used for firing, or baking, clay pots.

lost wax A method of casting bronze by melting wax in a mould and replacing it with molten metal.

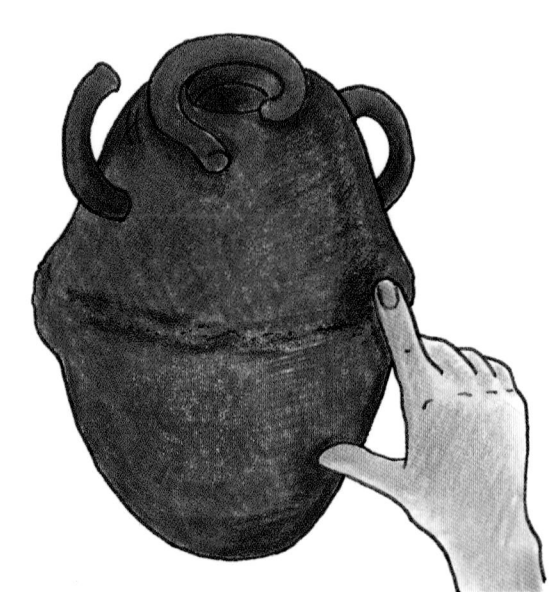

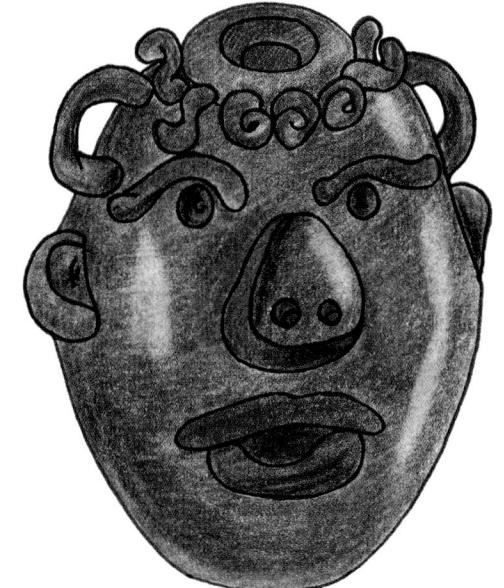

mint A place where metal coins are made.

mortar A mixture of lime with cement, sand and water, used in building and mosaic work.

mosaic The art of making a picture or design with small pieces of coloured material such as stone. The picture is also called a mosaic.

papyrus A reed plant that grows beside rivers.

plaque A flat piece of wood, metal or stone that is decorated or inscribed.

relief A sculpture in which figures or designs stand out from the background.

republic A state where the people elect representatives to run their government.

rite A solemn religious ceremony or act.

senate The state council of the Roman republic and empire.

signet ring A finger ring with a small seal.

suckle To give milk to a baby.

tableware Dishes, plates, glasses and other items used at meals.

terracotta Unglazed hard-baked clay used to make pottery objects.

toga A loose robe worn in ancient Rome.

vessel A hollow container, especially for holding liquids.

Index

amphorae 20, 22
archaeologists 9
Augustus 4, 6, 7

Bacchus 12
British Museum 25
bronze 6, 18, 19

cameos 27
chariots 21, 25
clay 18, 20, 21, 22, 25
coins 19, 27
Colchester 25
columns 7, 8, 9
Cupid 6

Dionysus 12

empire 4, 5, 6, 7, 8

figurines 18
frescoes 12, 13
friezes 8, 9
furniture 18, 19

gems 26-27, 28
gladiators 9
glass 14, 24-25, 26
gold 19, 26, 27, 28
gorgons 10
Greeks 6, 8, 12, 14,
   20, 26

hoards 27
Hoxne 27

jars 20
jewellery 26-27, 28
jugs 20
Julius Caesar 4, 19
Juno 19
Jupiter 19

lamps 20, 21
lost-wax method 18

marble 6, 7, 8
Marcus Aurelius 18
Mars 4
masks 20
Mesopotamia 14
metalwork 18-19
mint 19
money 19
mosaics 14-15, 16, 24
moulds 20, 25
myths and legends 8,
   12, 19

olive oil 20, 21

painting 12, 13
Pompeii 12, 14, 28
portraits 12, 27
pottery 20-21

reliefs 8, 9, 10, 21
Remus 4, 5
republic 4
Rhea Silvia 4
Rome 4, 5, 6, 7, 8, 12, 18,
   19, 21, 24, 25
Romulus 4, 5

sculpture 6-7, 8-9, 18
silver 19, 26, 27
statues 6, 7, 18

temples 7, 19
terracotta 5, 20, 21
tesserae 14
Tiber 4
tools 18

vases 20, 22, 24, 25
Vesuvius 12, 13

wall paintings 12-13, 14
wax 18
weapons 18
wolf 5